THE FIRST
MOON LANDING

BY DUCHESS HARRIS, JD, PHD
WITH ARNOLD RINGSTAD

Core Library

Cover image: Neil Armstrong photographed Buzz
Aldrin on the moon.

An Imprint of Abdo Publishing
abdopublishing.com

abdopublishing.com

Published by Abdo Publishing, a division of ABDO, PO Box 398166, Minneapolis, Minnesota 55439. Copyright © 2019 by Abdo Consulting Group, Inc. International copyrights reserved in all countries. No part of this book may be reproduced in any form without written permission from the publisher. Core Library™ is a trademark and logo of Abdo Publishing.

Printed in the United States of America, North Mankato, Minnesota
032018
092018

Cover Photo: Neil Armstrong/NASA
Interior Photos: Neil Armstrong/NASA, 1; JSC/NASA, 4–5, 30, 32–33, 36, 39, 43; Zaytseva Darya/Shutterstock Images, 9; Courtesy MIT Museum, 12–13; Retro Space Images/NASA, 18–19; NASA, 23 (left), 23 (right), 24–25; MSFC/ZumaPress/Newscom, 29

Editor: Marie Pearson
Imprint Designer: Maggie Villaume
Series Design Direction: Ryan Gale

Library of Congress Control Number: 2017962650

Publisher's Cataloging-in-Publication Data

Names: Harris, Duchess, author. | Ringstad, Arnold, author.
Title: The first moon landing / by Duchess Harris and Arnold Ringstad.
Description: Minneapolis, Minnesota : Abdo Publishing, 2019. | Series: Perspectives on American progress | Includes online resources and index.
Identifiers: ISBN 9781532114908 (lib.bdg.) | ISBN 9781532154737 (ebook)
Subjects: LCSH: Space ships--Juvenile literature. | Lunar landing sites--Juvenile literature. | Space flight to the moon--History--Juvenile literature. | Space race--Juvenile literature.
Classification: DDC 629.454--dc23

CONTENTS

THE CHALLENGE

On May 25, 1961, President John F. Kennedy walked into the halls of US Congress. He had an important mission. His goal was to convince the country to go to the moon.

Kennedy wanted the United States to be a leader in space. He wanted to set new goals for space exploration. This meant seeking funding from Congress. Kennedy's biggest goal was to land a man on the moon during the 1960s and then bring him back. This would be a huge task. But the audience liked Kennedy's message. Congress approved the spending. The quest for the moon had begun.

John F. Kennedy's speech encouraged NASA workers to make his vision of reaching the moon a reality.

The Space Race

The United States and the Soviet Union were in a heated competition. It became known as the space race. Each country wanted to prove it had better technology. Rockets could lift spacecraft into orbit.

The achievement made a statement about a country's military because the same rockets could carry bombs. Space technology was also military technology.

The space race had begun in October 1957. The Soviet Union launched the world's first satellite. It was called *Sputnik*. The spacecraft was only the size of a beach ball. But launching it was an impressive feat. The United States worked hard to catch up. It created the National Aeronautics and Space Administration (NASA) in 1958.

By 1961 the Soviet Union was still ahead. Yuri Gagarin became the first person in space on April 12. US astronaut Alan Shepard flew weeks later. His flight lasted just 15 minutes. This was all the space experience NASA had when Kennedy made his bold challenge.

Shepard's flight showed astronauts

CIVIL RIGHTS

President Kennedy's vice president was Lyndon B. Johnson, who saw a connection between the space program and civil rights. Many NASA facilities were in the South. In the 1960s, segregation and discrimination were severe in this part of the country. Johnson felt this was partly because the region was so poor. Johnson believed that going to the moon would create many skilled, high-paying jobs. He hoped that improving the economy would help advance civil rights, too.

could survive in space. Next came the Gemini program. Astronauts practiced steps needed for the moon landing program: Apollo.

Apollo

Each Apollo moon landing had the same basic plan. Three astronauts would climb into a cone-shaped ship. This was the command module. Attached to it was the service module. The service module supplied air, water, and electricity. It also had a large rocket engine. The key to the mission was the lunar module. This spiderlike craft had four legs. It had two rocket engines. One slowed the ship for landing. The other lifted the astronauts off the moon. Together, the three modules were called the Apollo spacecraft.

A massive Saturn V rocket boosted the Apollo spacecraft toward the moon. The trip took three days. In the moon's orbit, the astronauts split up. Two went into the lunar module. One stayed behind in the command module. The pair in the lunar module landed

STEPS IN A LUNAR
MISSION

There are many steps to a successful lunar mission. Look at these steps carefully. What would happen if one of them was left out?

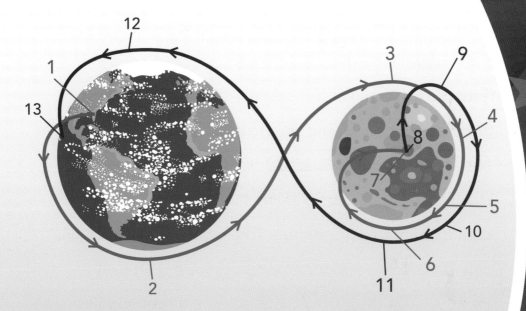

Outbound

1. Spacecraft launches
2. Spacecraft leaves Earth's orbit
3. Spacecraft slows down and enters Lunar orbit
4. Command module (CM) and Lunar module (LM) separate
5. CM orbits moon
6. LM descends
7. LM lands

Inbound

8. LM launches
9. CM and LM connect
10. Astronauts enter CM; LM is left behind
11. CM leaves Lunar orbit
12. CM reenters Earth's orbit
13. CM lands

on the moon. When they were ready to leave, they launched back into lunar orbit. The astronauts reunited in the command module. Then they used the service module's engine to boost themselves back to Earth. A few days later, they arrived home. Parachutes carried the command module to a safe landing in the ocean.

The Landing

The first mission to land on the moon was Apollo 11. Neil Armstrong and Buzz Aldrin were in the lunar module *Eagle*. Michael Collins stayed behind in the command module *Columbia*. The astronauts landed on July 20, 1969.

After the mission, the astronauts became celebrities. They went on a world tour. Huge crowds cheered for them. But Armstrong, Aldrin, and Collins were not the only people responsible for the achievement. Hundreds of thousands of people worked on the Apollo program. Each person had a unique perspective on the first moon landing.

STRAIGHT TO THE
SOURCE

On September 12, 1962, Kennedy gave a speech in Houston, Texas, home to a major NASA center. Kennedy explained why the country should take on his moon challenge:

> But why, some say, the moon? Why choose this as our goal? And they may well ask why climb the highest mountain? Why, 35 years ago, fly the Atlantic? . . . We choose to go to the moon. We choose to go to the moon in this decade and do the other things, not because they are easy, but because they are hard, because that goal will serve to organize and measure the best of our energies and skills, because that challenge is one that we are willing to accept, one we are unwilling to postpone, and one which we intend to win, and the others, too.

> Source: "John F. Kennedy Moon Speech—Rice Stadium." *Johnson Space Center.* NASA, n.d. Web. Accessed October 22, 2017.

Back It Up
In his speech, Kennedy is using reasons to support his argument. Explain the argument he is making. Then write down two or three reasons Kennedy provides.

PROGRAMMING APOLLO

The Apollo spacecraft was a complicated machine. Flying it to the moon was a task people once thought impossible. NASA realized it would need a computer. The computer would help keep the ship pointed in the right direction. It would control the spacecraft's rocket engines. The machine would be called the Apollo Guidance Computer (AGC). Margaret Hamilton was one of the pioneers behind the AGC.

Joining the Team

In 1964, Hamilton heard that the Massachusetts Institute of Technology (MIT) was working on Apollo software. This new project was

Margaret Hamilton stands by the software code she helped write that guided the spacecraft to the moon.

exciting to her. She had a background in math and computer science, so she called MIT and asked to join the team. Hamilton had an interview there the same day. She impressed the team leaders, and she got the job.

Hamilton led a team that developed AGC software. They were pioneers. They had to be. The field of software engineering was new. The team invented its own solutions to new problems. They faced a lot of pressure. The astronauts' lives would depend on their work. Hamilton thought about what would happen if there were a disaster in space. She later remembered, "I was always imagining headlines in the newspapers, and they would point back to how it happened, and it would point back to me."

Hamilton was interested in reliable software. Reliable software is designed to keep working no matter what. If it runs into errors, it knows how to solve the problem and continue. Software for life-or-death situations such as guiding a spacecraft must be reliable.

The Big Day

Hamilton was at MIT during the Apollo 11 landing. She was focused on software. Her team was listening to the radio link between the astronauts and Mission Control. They were ready to help if anything went wrong.

Suddenly a voice on the radio mentioned an alarm. It was a program alarm. The error code was 1201.

The computer was telling the astronauts something was going wrong. Hamilton looked across the room at another programmer. Their minds raced to figure out the problem.

They soon realized what was happening. The 1201 alarm meant the computer was overloaded with work. But the reliability features of the software were kicking in. When it was overloaded, the computer cleared out all of its work. Then it restarted. It allowed only the most important calculations to continue. The team at MIT heard Mission Control figure this out at

HAMILTON HONORED

Hamilton continues to be recognized for her work on Apollo. In November 2016 she was honored by President Barack Obama. He awarded her the Presidential Medal of Freedom. This is the highest civilian award given by the US government. Obama spoke at a ceremony honoring Hamilton and other recipients. He talked about the Apollo 11 mission. He said, "Our astronauts didn't have much time, but thankfully they had Margaret Hamilton."

the same time. Instead of aborting the landing, Mission Control let the astronauts keep going. Soon *Eagle* was sitting safely on the moon. Hamilton's reliable software had helped make the landing possible.

FURTHER EVIDENCE

Chapter Two discusses Margaret Hamilton and her work on the Apollo program. What was one of the main points of this chapter? What evidence is included to support this point? Read the interview with Hamilton at the website below. Does the information on the website support the main point of the chapter? Does it provide new evidence?

MARGARET HAMILTON INTERVIEW
abdocorelibrary.com/first-moon-landing

MAKING A MOON LANDER

To land on the moon, NASA would need a spacecraft unlike anything that came before. The lunar module would carry astronauts to the moon's surface. Then it would need to launch them back into orbit. Reliability was critical. The astronauts' lives depended on it. Tom Kelly and his team at the Grumman Aircraft Engineering Corporation, based on Long Island in New York, were up to the challenge.

As Tom Kelly, *front,* and his team designed the spacecraft, they also influenced the steps in the mission.

Early Work

First the engineers worked out the basic design. The lunar module would have two parts. The bottom would be the descent stage. It held a rocket engine and fuel tanks. It also included four landing legs. The descent stage engine would lower the spacecraft to the moon's surface.

The top of the lunar module would be the ascent stage. This section carried the astronauts. Controls would let them steer the lander. Windows would let them see outside. The ascent stage would also have its own rocket engine. When the astronauts were ready to leave the moon, the ascent stage would fire and lift them back to orbit. The descent stage would act as a launch pad. It would stay behind on the moon.

Engineering Challenges

The general design was ready. But there was still a lot of work to do to overcome thousands of engineering challenges. Kelly and his team worked to turn their drawings into reality.

Weight was one big issue. The spacecraft needed to be light. More weight meant more fuel would be needed to launch from Earth. But that fuel would add even more weight. The team struggled to trim pounds from the delicate spacecraft.

An engineer came up with a clever solution. He pointed at the seats in the lunar module design. He asked if they were really needed. Could the astronauts just stand? Standing would not be difficult in low gravity. It would also put the astronauts' eyes closer

KENNEDY KILLED

On November 22, 1963, President Kennedy was shot and killed in Dallas, Texas. The nation was stunned. Many Grumman employees went home for the day. But Kelly found an engineer waiting for him in his office. He needed Kelly to sign off on an updated diagram. Kelly remembered that the engineer told him, "Because President Kennedy himself set the schedule deadline for this project, he would want us to keep pushing ahead."

to the windows. This meant smaller windows could be used. This would save even more weight. Kelly studied the new drawings. The new windows were small triangles. A system of cables would help hold the standing astronauts steady during landing. The design worked.

Eagle Spreads Its Wings

On the day of the landing, Kelly was in the spacecraft analysis (SPAN) room at Mission Control. The mood was tense. The astronauts were having trouble. Their computer was displaying program alarms. Kelly and his team listened as Mission Control worked the

DESIGNING A LUNAR MODULE

These images show an early lunar module design, *left*, and the final lunar module. What changes can you find that are mentioned in the text? What other differences do you see?

problem. They soon determined the moon landing could continue.

When the astronauts landed safely, cheers went up in the SPAN room. The engineers there had dedicated years to this project. That long effort had finally succeeded. Kelly remembered his feelings at the time: "Seven years we had worked for this moment; how marvelous to experience it!"

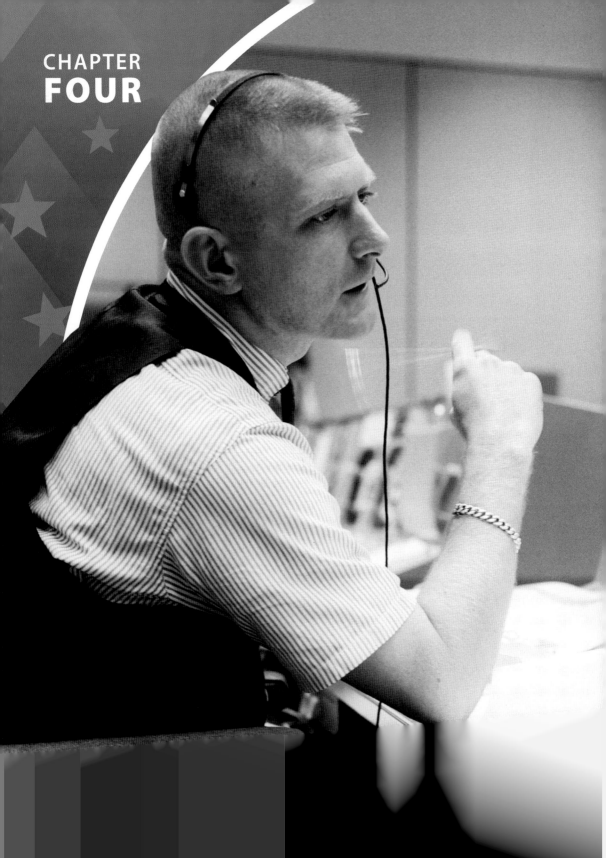

HELP FROM HOUSTON

The astronauts were the stars of the early space program. But they could not complete their missions alone. They needed support from the ground. This was where Mission Control came in. Workers in Mission Control were called flight controllers. They monitored the spacecraft from the ground. They spoke to the astronauts over the radio. They helped solve problems. The flight director was the leader of Mission Control. Each mission had several flight directors. The role rotated between them. Gene Kranz was one of these flight directors.

At 35 years old, Gene Kranz was one of the oldest people in Mission Control. The average age was 26.

Apollo 1

On January 27, 1967, Kranz was training with the Mission Control team for Apollo 1. After a long day, he finally went home. Others kept working. Kranz was planning to go out to dinner with his wife, Marta. Suddenly, he got news of a serious problem at NASA.

Kranz rushed back to Mission Control. The flight controllers were devastated. The three Apollo 1 astronauts had died. They were in the command module for testing. A fire broke out, and they could not escape.

The next morning, Kranz gathered the flight controllers.

PERSPECTIVES

A MISSION CONTROL TRADITION

Kranz's wife, Marta, helped create a Mission Control tradition. Starting with Gemini 4, she sewed him a new vest for each mission. "Gene wanted some kind of symbol for his team to rally around," Marta remembered. "I suggested a vest." The vests became famous at Mission Control. Kranz's Apollo 11 vest was white with fine silver thread.

He spoke to them about fixing the mistakes that had been made. Kranz was determined to not let something like the Apollo 1 disaster happen again.

Training for the Moon

In May 1969, Kranz and his team prepared for Apollo 11. The flight controllers sat in their places in Mission Control. The astronauts were in a training version of the spacecraft. A person called the simulation supervisor (SIMSUP) controlled the training. He could trigger problems in the mission. Mission Control and the astronauts had to work together to solve them.

The astronauts prepared to practice landing. Suddenly a computer alarm appeared. It was a 1201 alarm. The SIMSUP had triggered it. No one knew what it meant. Kranz decided to abort the mission. In real life, an abort was a risky decision. The astronauts would separate the ascent and descent stages while still high over the lunar surface. They would have to fly the ascent stage back to the command module.

NASA DRIVES PROGRESS

NASA employment efforts helped push back against discrimination and improve surrounding communities. The agency refused to use segregated facilities. This meant many hotels and convention centers near NASA centers were forced to integrate. NASA also hired people such as Charles Smoot. Smoot's job was to recruit black engineers and scientists to work for NASA. He worked with universities around the country to find talented individuals who could help drive the Apollo program forward. When these people moved to be near NASA centers in the South, they helped improve the communities where they lived and worked.

Afterward the SIMSUP was furious. The 1201 alarm had not been a serious problem. It simply meant the computer was overloaded. If nothing else went wrong, the landing could continue normally. They should not have aborted. Kranz spoke to Steve Bales, a computer expert on his team. He told Bales to write out a list of computer alarms. The list would include notes saying which ones were

Charles Smoot traveled the nation to find black scientists and encourage them to work for NASA.

serious and which were not. This would help the team act fast in a real mission. They wouldn't have to spend time looking up the alarms in thick manuals. Instead they could quickly refer to Bales's list.

The Landing

As Armstrong and Aldrin neared the surface, Aldrin's voice came in over the radio. There was a program

Mission Control celebrated when the Apollo 11 mission ended with success.

alarm, code 1202. Most people in the room did not know what it meant. Kranz turned to Bales. They recognized it as similar to the alarm from the simulation.

Bales called out, "We're go on that alarm." Kranz approved the crew to continue with the landing. Aldrin soon spoke again. There was another alarm. This time it was a 1201. Bales quickly responded, "Go . . . same type . . . we're go."

The descent continued. Flight controllers watched the lander's fuel levels. Time was running out. Finally *Eagle* reached the surface. Armstrong confirmed they had landed. Kranz was overcome with emotion. He couldn't speak. The first moon landing was a success. Teamwork and training had made it possible.

EXPLORE ONLINE

Chapter Four discusses the computer alarms that Kranz and his team dealt with during the first moon landing. The video on the website below covers the tense landing. How does the video help you better understand this event?

A TENSE LUNAR LANDING
abdocorelibrary.com/first-moon-landing

ONE SMALL STEP

More than 400,000 people worked on the Apollo program. Only a few would actually walk on the moon. Neil Armstrong was the first. He was a skilled pilot. Unlike some astronauts, he was not flashy. Armstrong was quiet and thoughtful. On Apollo 11, he would get the first chance to land on the moon.

Neil Armstrong, *left*, Michael Collins, *center*, and Buzz Aldrin each had their own jobs on the spacecraft.

The Descent

Armstrong and Aldrin had left Michael Collins behind. They were on their own now in the lunar module. The two astronauts attached the cables that would keep them steady. Then they fired the spacecraft's rocket engine. They began to slow down and descend toward the surface. The feeling of movement was not dramatic. It felt like going down an elevator.

As they made their descent, the astronauts remained calm as Mission Control instructed them to ignore the two warning alarms and to continue the landing. Armstrong looked outside as the lander descended. Aldrin watched the computer. He called out speed and altitude numbers. The alarms did not worry Armstrong. The spacecraft's controls were still responding normally. There did not seem to be any other problems.

Taking Control

The lunar module's computer was steering the spacecraft. But Armstrong did not recognize the landscape outside. They were far from their planned landing area. The computer was steering the spacecraft into a boulder field. Some of the rocks were the size of cars. It was an unsafe place to land.

Armstrong took manual control. He used a small joystick to steer the ship. He moved away from the boulders and searched for a better spot.

Next to him, Aldrin called out, "Quantity light." A light had turned on in the cabin. It showed that the

fuel was down to 5 percent. They would need to touch down soon.

Finally Armstrong found a flat area. He eased the lunar module down to the surface. The ship's engine kicked up dust below. The dust shot outward in fine sheets along the ground. This made it tough to see the surface. Armstrong lowered the ship further. Then he shut off the engine. *Eagle* gently settled to the lunar surface.

Everything went quiet. Armstrong and Aldrin turned to each other. They shook hands and patted each other on the shoulders. They had become the first humans on the moon.

First Steps

A few hours later, they prepared to walk outside. Armstrong would be first. They sealed up their suits. Then they emptied the air out of the cabin.

Collins orbited the moon in *Columbia*, waiting for *Eagle* to bring Armstrong and Aldrin back from the moon's surface.

The astronauts opened the hatch. Armstrong began climbing down the ladder.

On his way down, he pulled a handle that turned on a television camera. Back on Earth, a worldwide audience watched him. Armstrong reached the lunar module's foot pad. Then he set his left foot on the surface of the moon. He said, "That's one small step for man, one giant leap for mankind." Aldrin soon joined him. The astronauts collected rocks and took photos. Approximately two and a half hours later, they returned to the lunar module.

Armstrong held the camera, so most photos from the Apollo 11 mission show the second man on the moon, Aldrin.

Back to Earth

Armstrong and Aldrin slept on the moon. Then they got ready for launch. Aldrin called out a countdown. Right on time, the ascent engine fired. *Eagle* rose into lunar orbit. It met up with *Columbia*. The three men returned to Earth on July 24. They splashed down safely in the Pacific Ocean. NASA had met Kennedy's challenge.

The Apollo 11 mission was a success in the space race. It was also an important moment in human history. For the first time, people had walked on another world. More Apollo missions followed. They stayed on the moon longer. They collected more rocks and soil. But Apollo 11 will always be remembered as an important first step. Teamwork by programmers, engineers, flight controllers, astronauts, and many others made the mission work.

STRAIGHT TO THE
SOURCE

Right after his famous "one small step" statement, Armstrong's next words on the moon's surface described what he was seeing and feeling:

> *The surface is fine and powdery. I can kick it up loosely with my toe. It does adhere in fine layers, like powdered charcoal, to the sole and sides of my boots. I only go in a small fraction of an inch, maybe an eighth of an inch [0.3 mm], but I can see the footprints of my boots and the treads in the fine, sandy particles. . . . There seems to be no difficulty in moving around— as we suspected. It's even perhaps easier than the simulations of one-sixth g that we performed in the various simulations on the ground. It's absolutely no trouble to walk around. . . . The descent engine did not leave a crater of any size. It has about 1 foot [0.3 m] clearance on the ground. We're essentially on a very level place here.*

> Source: "One Small Step." *Apollo Lunar Surface Journal.* NASA, 1995. Web. Accessed November 30, 2017.

What's the Big Idea?

What is Armstrong trying to communicate? Why might these have been some of his first words on the moon's surface? If you were making the first landing on the moon or another planet, what do you think your first words might be?

IMPORTANT
DATES

1957

The Soviet Union launches Sputnik, the first satellite, in October.

1961

The Soviet Union launches Yuri Gagarin, the first astronaut, on April 12. Alan Shepard becomes the first US astronaut a few weeks later. On May 25, President John F. Kennedy asks the nation to commit to a moon landing by the end of the decade.

1962

President Kennedy gives a speech about the Apollo program at Rice University in Texas on September 12.

1964

Margaret Hamilton joins the Apollo Guidance Computer project at MIT.

1967

The Apollo 1 fire kills three astronauts on January 27.

1969

On July 20, Neil Armstrong and Buzz Aldrin land on the moon. They return to Earth along with Michael Collins on July 24.

STOP AND
THINK

Surprise Me

Chapter Two discusses the computers of Apollo and the career of Margaret Hamilton. After reading it, what two or three facts about these topics did you find most surprising? Write a few sentences about each fact. Why did you find each fact surprising?

Dig Deeper

After reading this book, what questions do you still have about the first moon landing? With an adult's help, find a few reliable sources that can help you answer your questions. Write a paragraph about what you learned.

Take a Stand

Some people want to send astronauts back to the moon. Others want to send people to Mars. Still others think the country should spend less money on space exploration. Which position do you agree with most? Write a paragraph about your opinion. Be sure to include reasons to back up your position.

GLOSSARY

abort
to stop a mission in an emergency and return home

civilian
a person who is not a member of the military

discrimination
unfair treatment of a person based on race, sex, or other reasons

guidance
the process of steering a spacecraft and keeping it on course

lunar
related to the moon

module
a self-contained part of a spacecraft

monitor
to watch over

orbit
the path an object takes around a large body in space, such as a planet or moon

simulation
a training version of something meant to look and feel like the real thing

ONLINE
RESOURCES

To learn more about the first moon landing, visit our free resource websites below.

Visit **abdocorelibrary.com** for free Common Core resources for teachers and students, including vetted activities, multimedia, and booklinks, for deeper subject comprehension.

Visit **abdobooklinks.com** for free additional online weblinks for further learning. These links are routinely monitored and updated to provide the most current information available.

LEARN
MORE

Doudna, Kelly. *Space Exploration*. Minneapolis, MN: Abdo, 2017.

Gagne, Tammy. *Women in Earth and Space Exploration*. Minneapolis, MN: Abdo, 2017.

ABOUT THE
AUTHORS

Duchess Harris, JD, PhD

Professor Harris is the chair of the American Studies department at Macalester College and curator of the Duchess Harris Collection of ABDO books. She is the author and coauthor of recently released ABDO books including *Hidden Human Computers: The Black Women of NASA, Black Lives Matter,* and *Race and Policing.*

Before working with ABDO, she authored several other books on the topics of race, culture, and American history. She served as an associate editor for *Litigation News,* the American Bar Association Section of Litigation's quarterly flagship publication, and was the first editor in chief of *Law Raza,* an interactive online journal covering race and the law, published at William Mitchell College of Law. She has earned a PhD in American Studies from the University of Minnesota and a JD from William Mitchell College of Law.

Arnold Ringstad

Arnold Ringstad has written more than 70 books for students. He especially enjoys reading and writing about space exploration. Ringstad lives in Minnesota with his wife and their cat.

INDEX